# Ideas Plus

A Collection of Practical Teaching Ideas

Book Nineteen

Scarlet Letter p21

Murder Rue Morgue p35

National Council of Teachers of English
1111 W. Kenyon Road, Urbana, Illinois 61801-1096

Project Coordinator: Felice Kaufmann

Assistant Project Coordinator: Emily Nafziger

Copyeditor: Jane Curran

Cover Design and Interior Book Design: Tom Jaczak

Cover Photographs: James E. Corley and Thompson-McClellan Photography

NCTE Stock Number: 22833

Library of Congress Catalog Card Number 84-3479

*Ideas Plus* is published in the fall by the National Council of Teachers of English as an exclusive benefit of NCTE Plus membership. NCTE Plus membership also includes four issues of *Classroom Notes Plus* (ISSN 0738-86-24),
published in January, April, August, and October. Annual membership dues are
$60.00; $20.00 of this amount is for *Classroom Notes Plus* and *Ideas Plus*.
Inquiries about NCTE Plus membership or communications regarding change
of address and permission to reprint should be addressed to *Classroom Notes
Plus*, 1111 W. Kenyon Road, Urbana, IL 61801-1096. POSTMASTER: Send
address changes to *Classroom Notes Plus*, 1111 W. Kenyon Road, Urbana, IL
61801-1096. Second-class postage paid at Champaign, Illinois, and at additional mailing offices.

# Contents

# Foreword

*Ideas Plus* and its quarterly companion *Classroom Notes Plus* are the principal benefits of NCTE Plus membership.

The ideas collected in this nineteenth edition of *Ideas Plus* come from two sources: ideas submitted at an Idea Exchange session at an NCTE Annual Convention or Spring Conference and contributions by readers of *Classroom Notes Plus* and *Ideas Plus*.

Some of the teaching practices described here are innovative and surprising; others are adaptations on familiar ideas. Your own ingenuity will doubtless come in handy as you customize these approaches for your students.

Feel free to send us a teaching practice of your own to share with NCTE Plus members. Submissions for consideration may be mailed to *Ideas Plus/Classroom Notes Plus*, 1111 W. Kenyon Road, Urbana, IL 61801-1096; or sent by e-mail to notesplus@ncte.org.

# *1* PREWRITING AND WRITING

Staring at a blank sheet of white paper, doodling in the margins, studying the slow movement of the hands on the clock, sneaking a look at a classmate's paper—we've all watched students fidget when they were unable to transfer their ideas into words on the page, or even to come up with the ideas. The activities in this chapter will stimulate creative thinking and help your students express their thoughts in clear, precise language. Included are ideas that will encourage students to improve their fluency, use persuasive language, create dialogue for their characters, and step beyond their focus on themselves to recognize the impact that others have had on them.

## Exercises for Fluency

At the beginning of each school year I engage my students in a series of mini-lessons that plant the seeds and provide the tools for writing. Upon completion of these writing-readiness activities, my students have an "I can write" attitude. Though I use these activities with elementary students, they're useful and stimulating exercises that could be effective at any age and could be particularly helpful with ESL students or students who need additional practice using descriptive language.

How much time you spend on each of these exercises depends on the needs and the age of your students. I generally spend 15 to 30 minutes on each lesson and teach them sequentially over a period of two to three weeks.

### Rush, Rush, Rush (Part 1)

Rush, Rush, Rush is intended to create fluency in writing. The goal is quantity, not quality.

1. One student selects an object from a boxed collection I have assembled. That object becomes the writing topic for the entire class.
2. Students spend three minutes individually writing lists of words and phrases that come to mind when thinking about the selected object.
3. When time is up, students count the entries on their own lists and record the total at the top of the list. (The fact that we count and tally our words helps motivate students to write quickly and think of as many words as possible.)
4. Students then look for one word or phrase from their own list that they think no one else in the classroom has thought of.
5. Students share their selected words and phrases. Sometimes we comment on an unusual or unexpected word or a word that everyone has used.
6. I repeat this activity several times. The collected objects I've used have ranged from a piece of candy to a pillow. The possibilities are endless.

## Rush, Rush, Rush (Part 2)

This extension of the first exercise also seeks fluency, but this time students are asked to write sentences rather than words.

1. One student selects one item from the box to be a writing topic for the class.
2. Students spend three minutes individually writing sentences about the item.
3. Students count their sentences and write the total at the top of the page.
4. Students select their favorite sentence to read aloud and tell why they like it.
5. I repeat this activity several times.

## Words Come Alive

This exercise helps students learn how to choose vivid words instead of overused, trite words.

1. Students form small groups for this activity.
2. I give each group an index card that has a "plain" word written

on top. Plain words are overused words such as *good, beautiful, said, went, nice, happy*, etc.

3. Students replace each plain word with a more descriptive, vivid word. Each group brainstorms alternate words and writes them on a sheet of poster board.
4. Each group shares their words with the class and comments on why their words are an improvement over the original words.
5. I display the posters in the classroom as references.

## Write What You Mean

This exercise encourages the use of detail.

1. I prepare two short paragraphs: one in which several activities are described, but no descriptive adjectives or adverbs are used, and another version of the same paragraph in which descriptive words and phrases are included to paint a more vivid picture. For the first example, I use something like this:

> Yesterday I went to the park. I had fun. I stayed all day and then I went home and ate dinner.

2. I read the paragraph aloud and then ask the students to think about what is in their minds as I read. What pictures are they seeing? When students share ideas, the class discovers that some students had one idea of what was happening, some had another idea, and some usually say that they didn't have any visual image in their minds at all.
3. Next I read aloud the second version of the paragraph, which includes vivid descriptive adjectives and adverbs. For example:

> Yesterday I went to the city park that has the huge circular pond. I had fun splashing water all over my friends with an empty Coke can. I stayed all day until the sun went down and I got chilly. Then I went home and ate a big bowl of steaming soup to warm up.

4. Then I ask students what happens as they hear this version of the paragraph. Are the pictures in their minds more vivid? Which words and phrases help create a picture? How do the sensory details affect them as they listen? After comparing the two versions,

students readily understand that a writer who wants to convey a clear, vivid picture needs to use descriptive language and that sensory details are an important way to add interest to a piece of writing.

5. As a variation on this activity, I sometimes read the first paragraph and ask students to draw what they see. Then I do the same with the second, more descriptive version. This also can be an effective way to show students that descriptive language forms more detailed and vivid pictures in the mind.

## As What as a What?

The purpose of this exercise is to focus student attention on one useful type of figurative language, the simile.

1. Students sit in one large circle.
2. I state, "I have a dog as long as a limo."
3. Students reply, "As what as a what?"
4. I repeat my sentence.
5. Each student then takes a turn sharing a simile on any topic, and each time the rest of the circle responds, "As what as a what?" The creation and repetition of the many different similes help students feel comfortable creating and using their own similes in writing.

These simple exercises can help make your students ready, willing, and able to participate in the writing process throughout the school year.

*Judy E. Neal, Porter, Texas*

---

# "And Now for the Rest of the Story . . ."

---

I use the story of Goldilocks and the three bears to involve students in a mock-trial project that involves writing, speaking, role-playing, and using persuasive language. I originally got the idea for this assignment from a passage in the short story "Blues Ain't No Mockin' Bird" by Toni Cade Bambara, which presents a different perspective on the traditional story:

"I read a story once," said Cathy soundin like Granny teacher. "About this lady Goldilocks who barged into a house that wasn't even hers. And not invited, you understand. Messed over the people's groceries and broke up the people's furniture. Had the nerve to sleep in folks' bed."

First, I present students with an unbiased oral summary of the Goldilocks story, which simply describes the events up to the point where the bears return home. At this point, I stop and insert radio commentator Paul Harvey's famous phrase, "And now for the rest of the story. . . ." I continue: "As soon as Momma Bear noticed someone had eaten the porridge, she dialed 911. The police arrived just as Goldilocks ran out of the house. After a brief chase, the officers caught Goldilocks."

At this point, I start a discussion about the "evidence" against Goldilocks, and students help me compile information that can be used against her: the empty porridge bowl, the broken chair, Baby Bear's statement, and the statements of police officers who witnessed Goldilocks leaving the house.

I explain to students that we are going to hold a short trial for Goldilocks, and that they will need to take the part of key participants and write depositions for the court. I explain that a deposition is defined as either spoken or written testimony given under oath. Students or pairs of students volunteer to write depositions for Goldilocks, Momma Bear, Papa Bear, Baby Bear, the police officers, and Goldilocks's family.

Students have one class period to write their depositions and one class period to edit and polish them. During the next class period, students will be reading their statements to the judge (me), so I begin by giving them some tips on presentation techniques, such as the importance of speaking slowly and clearly, making occasional eye contact, and avoiding nervous gestures. While each student reads aloud his or her deposition, the other students take notes. I give a few tips on note-taking, too: listen for important points, don't try to write down every word, jot down key words and phrases, and use simple abbreviations for common words.

Then it's time for "closing arguments." Each student decides to be either a defense attorney or a prosecuting attorney, and as homework for the next class period they write short persuasive essays from the point of view of their chosen attorney. They are to rely on previous class discussions, the depositions they heard, persuasive language, and their own imaginations to try to convince the reader that Goldilocks is innocent or guilty. During the next class period, students meet in pairs to hold writing conferences and to revise and edit their short essays.

At the beginning of the final class, students are again grouped in pairs, with each pair consisting of one defense attorney and one prosecuting attorney. Each pair of students reads their arguments to the judge (me) and jury (their classmates), who vote whether Goldilocks is innocent or guilty based on the arguments just heard. We keep a running tally on the chalkboard, and the final count of court decisions determines her fate. (If there's a tie, the judge may determine whether to grant a reprieve or declare a mistrial.)

This project involves students in a variety of language activities, and students enjoy the twist it gives to a familiar story.

**Betty Geffers, Mount Pleasant Independent School District, Texas**

## From Word Bubbles to Written Dialogue

Here is an idea I have recently used to help my seventh graders develop a better understanding of how to write dialogue.

To prepare for this activity, I select, cut out, and photocopy two comic strips from the Sunday newspaper. Using white correction fluid, I cover the words in the dialogue bubbles on one copy of each cartoon. Then I make overhead transparencies of both versions of the two comics.

I also select five comic strips from the weekday edition of the newspaper, arrange them together on one 8 ½" x 11" sheet of paper, and go through the same process of photocopying, covering the dialogue bubbles on one copy, and making transparencies. I also make a photocopy of the blank version for each student.

In class I introduce my students to the concept of dialogue and how it is necessary to make a narrative really come to life. To illustrate this, I use the overhead projector to display the first blanked-out cartoon, and I call for volunteers to fill in the blanks. It is sometimes slow at first, but students usually warm up to the task quickly. I place a blank transparency over the cartoon on the overhead and write down the dialogue as students dictate it to me. (Sometimes the dialogue my students create is better than the dialogue the cartoonist came up with.)

I then put up the second blank transparency and have students write out a dialogue for it on their own. I circulate around the room to make sure everyone has the idea, and then we share our creations. Students are always interested to hear the different ways people interpret what is happening in the comic strip. For additional practice, I give each student a copy of the five blank strips to work on in class and, if necessary, to finish for homework.

The next step is to distribute guidelines for written dialogue (covering such points as using quotations marks at the beginning and end of each character's speech; using a period, exclamation point, or question mark at the end of each speech, inside the quotes; and starting a new paragraph with each change of speaker) and to transform one of the strips into a short written scene that includes dialogue. I have found it helpful to model this for students first—placing a comic strip with text on the overhead and going through the steps of turning it into a simple narrative with dialogue. I explain that anything that would be in a "word bubble" in the comic strip should be in quotation marks, and that instead of the bubble "pointing" to the speaker to show who's talking, we use "he said" or "she said" or similar verbs.

A recent suggestion from a colleague has provided a simple way of reminding students to start a new paragraph for each change of speaker. In my colleague's words, "new bubble = new paragraph."

*Art Belliveau, Russell County Middle School, Seale, Alabama*

---

# Honor Thy Classmate

How wonderful it would be if we started looking for the "good" in each person! How much better our world would be if we would focus on the positive! "Honor Thy Classmate" helps my students to do just that. I put all the names of my students in a bag. Each student selects the name of a fellow classmate and then writes a poem to honor him or her.

The form for the poem may be any that the student wishes to use. Many choose to use the bio-poem form, which is ordinarily used as a self-descriptive poem. The bio poem contains eleven lines. The first and last lines contain the person's first name and last name. In between, the writer includes some information about the chosen person. Here's the formula:

Line 1: First Name
Line 2: Traits (list four traits that describe this person)
Line 3: "Sibling of . . ." (description of sibling is optional)
Line 4: "Lover of . . ." (list four items)
Line 5: "Who needs . . ." (list three items)
Line 6: "Who gives . . ." (list three items)
Line 7: "Who feels . . ." (list three items)
Line 8: "Who fears . . ." (list three items)
Line 9: "Who would like to see . . ." (list three items)
Line 10: "Resident of . . ." (name of a place)
Line 11: Last Name

Students are to give me their framed poems two days before the "reading" and must not reveal the identity of their subjects. Excitement fills the room when the day comes for my students to read their poems. Students have heard from previous classes what a special assignment this is, and they are eager to hear the descriptions of their classmates. Some of the best poems have been written by students who selected names of classmates that they did not know well. They had to become detectives and search for information to use for their poems and many times have discovered how special their subjects really were.

Here is an excerpt from one student's finished poem:

To Rachel
Your friends are lucky to have someone like you.
Someone who is always honest and true.
When people are lost you show them the way.
You always seem to have the right words to say.
Never change because your life has just begun to start.
Keep living your life to its fullest,
and always follow your heart.
—from Michael

**Susan Smith Akin, Pinson Valley High School, Pinson, Alabama**

## A Medley of Writing Starts

I have pulled together these teaching methods by combining the suggestions and strategies of many different teachers. The idea for the "writing start" came from Dr. Marie Nelson at the University of

Florida. The specific plan for "read-around-groups" mentioned here came from Beverly Jones at Fort Clarke Middle School in Gainesville, Florida. All other ideas are original.

Helping students become better communicators is the main goal of my language arts class. Reading, writing, speaking, listening, and viewing are the ways that we communicate in society, and language arts classes tackle all five areas.

Although I teach all these aspects of communication throughout the year in many different ways, I have developed a weekly staple for my class that combines all five and brings students in touch with a variety of stimuli from the "real" world outside of school. My students know it as the "writing start."

Most language arts classes have a day for writing in journals or responding in writing to prompts or stimuli. The writing start is similar; students must write at least half of a page each Thursday in response to the prompt that I give them, and they receive a grade for the assignment each week. It is called a "writing start" because students may use the writing as a first draft or prewrite for our longer writing assignments. The types of prompts that I give and what we do with the writing when it is completed are the unique aspects of this teaching strategy. I try to present students with many different types of stimuli, and I give them options for how they may respond.

One time we discussed how wonderful writing can inspire works of art, and how beautiful art can inspire people to write. I read aloud a passage by J. R. R. Tolkien that had inspired a painting as I projected a copy of the painting on the wall. I then projected another painting and asked the students to let it inspire them as they wrote.

In another response to art, I projected a painting by an African American artist who lives in Atlanta and asked students either to imagine what had inspired him or to write about what they saw in the painting.

Before Halloween, I brought in *The Pop-Up Book of Phobias* by Gary Greenberg (Rob Weisbach Books, 1999), a book with pop-up pictures of the most common phobias and explanations for each picture. They included arachnophobia, with a large, realistic-looking spider popping up out of the book. After students heard and viewed this book, their assignment was to write about what they fear.

Before Thanksgiving, I read excerpts from a cookbook with mouth-watering pictures of food. For this assignment, the students either wrote recipes or described their holiday traditions.

In January, I read them the true story of a man who had written down over one hundred goals for his life when he was a teenager and was close to meeting them by the time he was forty-seven. Their assignment was to try writing fifteen goals for their own life, steering away from material possessions.

Most recently, as part of our poetry unit, we discussed the difference between reading the lyrics to a song and listening to the song being sung. I first read aloud the lyrics to a favorite song of mine, and then we listened to the song several times as they wrote either about how the two experiences were different, or about whether it is the lyrics or the sound of the music that determines why they like music on the radio.

The different stimuli I use result in a wide variety of responses. What do I do with these wonderful responses?

Each Friday following the prompt, we do one of three activities. Some days we have read-around-groups. On these days, students get into groups of three or four. Each group has a letter, and each student has a number. Students write their group letter and their number on their papers rather than their names. Each group exchanges its papers with the students in another group and spends two to four minutes silently reading the papers it receives.

When time is up, the group members must discuss and agree on which paper is the best in the batch; they write down the number and letter of that paper. The process continues until every student has read every paper.

When students have their own papers back, I tally the votes, and the "winners" from each group are revealed. In order to earn the extra points that this honor conveys, the winners must read their writing starts aloud to the class.

The listening classmates must follow presentation etiquette, meaning that they must listen attentively and quietly, and they clap when the presentation is finished. They are allowed to ask any reasonable questions of the speaker, and the speaker answers.

Although I did not develop the idea of read-around-groups, I have made some changes so that the groups fit perfectly with what the writing starts are meant to accomplish. Unfortunately, the read-around-groups do not allow every student to speak in front of the class. This problem led to our other two Friday activities.

Some days, we play the game "spin-the-pen." We get into one big circle with writing starts in hand. I place a pen in the middle of the circle, spin it, and if the designated end lands pointing to a student, that student has to stand up and read. The good news for these students is that this will earn them bonus points. The game usually continues until everyone has read, or until class ends.

On our busier Fridays, students have the opportunity to stand up and share by volunteering. On these days, anyone who volunteers gets the bonus points. The methods of sharing that I use with writing starts are effective on all fronts of the language arts spectrum.

I give students a way to respond to what they view and hear, and they form a much more positive attitude toward writing when they are interested in the topic. They also write knowing that their papers may be read and heard by peers, and they adjust their writing accordingly.

When they do read one another's papers, they improve their judgment skills and their own ways of writing, and during the times when we share writings, they are practicing both their public-speaking skills and their skills as audience members. I would certainly recommend this approach to any middle school language arts teacher.

*Laurie A. Dennison, South Paulding Middle School, Dallas, Georgia*

---

# My Book of Others

Imagine your eighth graders crowded around your desk one morning, excited about a project they were turning in and eager to see what others had created. This teacher's fantasy became a reality through the project I call "My Book of Others."

As Lois Lowry, author of *The Giver,* wrote, "And if I've learned anything, it is that we can't live in a walled world, in an 'only us, only now' world." None of us is an island—instead, we all live in a social world where others impact our lives, contributing to who we are and who we will become.

"My Book of Others" encourages students to honor those with whom they are journeying through life. The total booklet consists of 10 separate pages, each with its own creative focus and writing challenge.

## Page One

Page one stresses "Honoring Others." Students are to imagine that they have just written their first novel. They then write a brief dedication to a special person. To better understand the format, we read some dedications by published authors before students start writing.

## Page Two

Page two, "Learning from Others," focuses on early mentors (day-care personnel, preschool or kindergarten teachers). I first share with the students some basic lessons from Robert Fulghum's *All I Really Need to Know I Learned in Kindergarten* (Fawcett, 1993). Then they write about five early lessons they learned and how these lessons still impact their lives today.

Lessons learned range from recognizing that crayons are for drawing, not eating, to realizing that "LMNOP" is not one single letter in the alphabet, and to understanding the value of the "friendship circle." The accounts are both humorous and touching.

## Page Three

On page three, "Reaching Out to Others," students pretend they have just won a million dollars on "Who Wants to Be a Millionaire?" There's a catch, however: they have to become philanthropists and give away all of their money. Students' choice of recipients and their explanations reveal much about the students and their hearts of gold.

## Page Four

The fourth page emphasizes "Thanking a Special Other." Using the correct form for a friendly letter, they write to a middle school teacher who most positively affected them, both academically and personally. (I encourage them to select someone other than me, though I don't actually restrict their choice.) Several colleagues told me they had tears in their eyes as they read letters by former and current students.

## Page Five

"Getting to Know a Special Other" results in a fascinating page five. Students interview an adult who plays a role in their world but about whom they know very little: a neighbor, a bus driver, a salesperson at their favorite store, a coach or dance teacher, a librarian, a waitress at their favorite restaurant, a nurse or receptionist, etc. This helps students develop respect for others and a better understanding of the many jobs involved in helping our communities run smoothly. Students write up their interviews in dialogue format.

## Page Six

Page six combines U.S. history with language arts. In "Electing a Presidential Other," students write a campaign speech for a friend or relative who they believe would make the ideal U.S. president. They are asked to think about qualities they think are necessary to be a good president and to make their choice accordingly. They must also mention in their speeches the issues they believe are important for a president to address.

## Page Seven

My students' favorite was page seven: "An Ideal Microcosm of Others." I ask students to think about their friends (who may or may not be students at our school) and the strongest characteristics and qualities of these friends. Then students are to think about the classes they are currently taking, both core classes and electives. Their assignment is to create the ideal staff of teachers for these classes by assigning a friend to teach each class. Students must explain why the characteristics and qualities of each person make him or her a good fit for the job. Students' writings for this page can be very imaginative, and sometimes quite humorous.

## Page Eight

For page eight, "Painting a Picture of an Important Other," students write a creative poem about a special person in their lives. We use an 11-line format for our poems, but other forms of poetry could be used as well.

## Page Nine

The eighth-grade core novel for our school is *To Kill a Mockingbird*. For page nine, "In the Eyes of Others," I make reference to Atticus

Finch's advice and ask students to step into another's shoes to better understand themselves. Students are asked to choose three adjectives they feel others would use to describe them. They also need to include a specific example from their lives to support each adjective. This step has produced some delightful writings.

## Page Ten

The "Book of Others" ends with the tenth page, "A Recipe from Others." Using cooking terms, the students write a recipe that creatively shows the ingredients others in their lives have given to them.

The final product, including a cover collage of pictures of others, a title page, and the 10 polished pages, is a masterpiece of creativity and caring. Many students laminated each page, used computer paper that captured the theme of each focus, and added graphics, pictures, or their own illustrations. All booklets were beautifully bound. I set up this assignment so that each written page was worth nine points, with the cover and title page worth five points each. Many students received extra credit for their extraordinary efforts.

As my eighth graders prepare to enter the larger world of high school, "My Book of Others" reminds them that they are not alone. No matter what challenges await them, they will always have other people supporting them and applauding them.

*Ronna L. Edelstein, Abbott Middle School, West Bloomfield, Michigan*

# 2 LITERATURE

The written word is alive and well, although it can be difficult to convince students that this is the case. After all, there's no remote control for a novel. With so many forms of visual entertainment available to our students, we need to encourage them to read often and to read with involvement. By filling our classrooms with attractive and inviting books and by utilizing activities that stimulate and challenge students, we demonstrate how literature can enrich our lives by introducing us to new worlds and new ideas. The teaching ideas in this chapter offer numerous ways to combine critical thinking and the reading of novels, short stories, and poetry. Included are activities that focus on the point of view of the characters in *The Scarlet Letter,* examine literary elements in songs such as "The Distance" by Cake, award Oscars to characters and events in *Animal Farm,* and help Huck Finn sing the blues.

## Imaginative Responses to *The Scarlet Letter*

In conjunction with our class study of *The Scarlet Letter,* we offer students a choice of four writing assignments to encourage them to think more deeply about the characters and themes. We distribute the following information in handout form.

### Student Handout

In *The Scarlet Letter,* Hawthorne introduces us to some interesting aspects of society and some characters toward whom we have strong feelings. Think about how you feel toward the characters and their actions and then choose one of the following writing options. Your essay should be two double-spaced typed pages in length, or approximately 500 words.

1. Most of this story is told from the point of view of the author, Nathaniel Hawthorne. Rewrite *The Scarlet Letter* in the format of a short story, but this time take the point of view of one of the following characters: Hester Prynne, Roger Chillingworth, or Arthur Dimmesdale. Be sure to stay true to the plot and to the Puritan setting.

2. What kind of a woman do you imagine Pearl, the "demon-child," became? Did she really marry royalty and live happily ever after? Write the story of one or more incidents in Pearl's life after she and Hester left their New England community. In your story, show how Pearl's early childhood experiences affect her as an adult and how she deals with her own strengths and weaknesses. You may write in first-person, using Pearl's voice, or you may write in third-person, using an outside narrator.

3. Hester has died. As a community member, you want to express your views about her life and her personal character. How do you feel about the community's treatment of her? How do you think she should be remembered? What lesson do you think the community could learn from Hester's story? Write a letter to the editor of the community newspaper, presenting your opinions of these points or points similar to these.

4. The story of *The Scarlet Letter* begins with Hester being led from prison to the scaffold, but what happened to get her into this situation (aside from the obvious)? This "secret life" before the story begins is truly a catalyst for everything that happens later. Write a diary of that "secret life." Your diary should be from Hester's perspective and should show how she went from a life of respectability to the life of shame and isolation you see in the story. Some possible diary entries might be: How did all of this begin between the two? Where did they first meet? What might Hester have been thinking? Are there circumstances that we don't know? Remember to keep in mind what happens in the story as well as the values and traditions of the time period.

We tell students that we will consider all of the following as we evaluate their work: clarifying the focus of the paper in the first paragraph; showing a clear understanding of the characters as they appeared in *The Scarlet Letter* by using references to the events in the story; maintaining an appropriate tone and mood throughout the writing, whether it be a short story, letter, or diary entry; including an appropriate and effective conclusion; and correct grammar, spelling, and use of verb tenses.

*Linda Mack Berlin and Melissa A. Schneider, Grandville High School, Grandville, Michigan*

# A Deeper Look at Songs and Poems

With careful planning and creative strategies, I use a spring poetry unit to transform my classroom into a verdant poetry garden, and my eighth graders come to understand what William Carlos Williams meant when he said: "It is difficult to get the news from poetry, yet every day men die miserably for lack of what is found there."

Just for fun, I begin my poetry unit with a chart on the board that compares the qualities of a poem—free form, emotional, exuberant, intensely sad or intensely happy, wild, silly, funny, passionate—to the typical teen, and even students agree that the two are strikingly similar.

Then I hook students into studying poetry by getting them to examine music lyrics. Any genre of contemporary music will do as long as it provides rich examples that underscore the goal of teaching literary elements. Students often begin by saying, "We don't listen to the words; the music is what counts." That is, until we start picking apart the poetry—the lyrics—and uncover the mystery of language.

For example, a song called "The Distance" by Cake appears to be about a guy running, and then attention shifts to a car in a race. Upon closer inspection, we discover that the song is really an allegory, using a race to symbolize how the man is trying to run away from his own guilt and grief over losing the woman he loves. Like peeling away thin layers of onion skin, we can find more meanings hidden in the language, and students clamor for more examples of allegory.

Here's what one student had to say about "The Distance":

"The Distance" is an example of how some songs aren't always what they seem. The phrase "Reluctantly crouched at the starting line, engines pumping and thumping at time" is a form of imagery, but it is deceiving. It makes you think it is about a race. But is it? Is it really about a race?

"He's going the distance, He's going for speed, She's all alone, all alone in her time of need." "The Distance" is an allegory, using the races and the cup to represent what is going on. It doesn't tell you directly; it makes you think. Another example that uses allegory is "Vincent." Listening to the lyrics to "The Distance" makes you think.

I can list many songs and poems that have a much deeper story line than what they make you think. "O' Captain my Captain" misleads you to think it is about a ship, when it is really about Lincoln. Knowing this, I now think harder when I listen or read a poem or song.

After class discussion of several examples of music lyrics, we move to an art project. Students select a song, copy the lyrics onto a sheet of poster paper, illustrate the song, and then present the poster to the class. Variations are possible, too. For instance, some students may prefer to work with a partner to create a slide show or a Power Point presentation illustrating the words of their chosen song. Sharing these projects with the class is a wonderful experience as students analyze and explain lyrics by their favorite artists.

The next step in the unit is to study some master poets of the modern age. We read works by such modern poets as Robert Frost, Walt Whitman, Gwendolyn Brooks, William Carlos Williams, Dylan Thomas, Gary Soto, and Langston Hughes. After students discuss, imitate, and write about these poets, they are ready to write their own poetry. Thorough exposure to good poetry seems to help inoculate them against trite phrases and rhyming without reason.

Our classroom editors then collect these poems for publication in our classroom literary magazine, *Élan*. Student artists prepare illustrations and do design work while circulation managers take orders and distribute. It is quite an operation as we produce a fuller, richer magazine each year.

I try to make sure all my students are featured in our magazine, through their poetry as well as through their artistic abilities and other skills. Students eagerly await the day *Élan* arrives hot off the press, and they gather in groups to read each other's poetry. We celebrate by converting the classroom into the Groovy Poetry Garden Coffee House. Parents are invited to come and hear the hip artists read poetry and play music.

This approach to poetry is a success for several reasons. First, students are hooked because they make connections with their world. Students learn about literary terms and language use through hands-on projects and begin to discuss theme, juxtaposition, and symbolism on their own. The rate for turning in projects is virtually 100 percent because students are so eager to share their work in our literary magazine.

Perhaps most importantly, when I bring out an unfamiliar poem for students to explore, they now approach it not with dread but with excitement. And I hope that maybe, just maybe, when they are rocking with their headphones on, they will be listening to the words as well as the music.

*Ann C. Federico, Hidden Oaks Middle School, Palm City, Florida*

# And the Winner Is . . .

I always enjoy reading other teachers' variations on the Oscar motif. Here is one that's as quick and simple as instant coffee and that's designed to keep the entire class participating. The boredom that goes with interminable Oscar presentations is avoided. I use this as the concluding exercise for *Animal Farm* with my eighth-grade class.

## Proposals

Students go to the board in groups of two or three to brainstorm for appropriate Oscars to be awarded for *Animal Farm*. When there are more listings than the number of students, the proposals are read aloud. Each student is randomly called to select the Oscar he or she will award. The 20 categories chosen this year included Most Animalistic, Most Powerful Phrase, Most Colorful Character, Most Chilling Moment, Strongest Antagonist, Most Descriptive Death, Most Beautiful Image, Funniest Animal, Biggest Heart, Best Song, Bravest Animal, and Best Adaptation of a Real Event.

## Nominations

Students are to take no more than a half page to list three nominations for their award, making the strongest case they can for each. I give students two days for this so they can think carefully about the best evidence and compose a concise supporting statement. The half page concludes with the naming of the winner. I ask for typed scripts and illustrations if possible; all neat awards will be displayed.

## Presentations

Students read aloud their nominations. Just after the third nomination is completed, I stop the reader and ask another student to state which nominee he or she would choose. Then the nominator names the actual winner. I allow the class to give a drum roll on their desks at the dramatic pause before the winner's name is announced.

### Sample Presentation for Most Chilling Scene

First there is the murder scene, where some of the animals confess to their "crimes," and the dogs attack and kill them. This scene is very disturbing because it breaks one of the Seven Commandments, "No animal shall kill another animal." Also, the description of the pile of dead animals produces an eerie feeling.

The second nominee is the scene when the pigs come out, all of them walking on their hind legs, with the sheep bleating, "Four legs good, two legs better." This goes against the whole concept of animalism.

The third nominee is the last scene in the book. The animals are looking through the window and see the pigs and men bonding, but when they look from pig to man, they are unable to tell the difference. This is really disturbing, because the pigs are so corrupt from their power that they have evolved into something else.

Now, dear reader, which scene would *you* give the award to? Ah, the confession and execution? You'll have to go to the end of the activity to learn the student's award.

## Commercials

Watching the clock carefully, I intersperse the awards with impromptu commercials. I have previously prepared 10 cards with product names on them, some real, some made-up, such as *Queen Cat Catnip and Tid-*

*bits, L. L. Bean's Plaid Fleece Blankets and Dog Beds, Pepsi, Milk,* and so on. I am prepared to present the first commercial to give students a model, but usually that is not necessary. When I announce that the commercials will be improvised by audience members, hands wave eagerly. I find that many students crave this opportunity to show their comic skills. This exercise takes exactly one class period, and I feel like a TV newscast director for making that happen. Students actively participate in the activity, and I have only to grade the nominations and display the neat ones on the bulletin board.

*And for those who are interested, the Most Chilling Scene Oscar went to the last scene in the book with the pigs and men.

**Rosemary Laughlin, University Laboratory High School, Urbana, Illinois**

# Examining Frederick Douglass and the American Dream

*The Narrative of the Life of Frederick Douglass, An American Slave,* when included as part of a unit on "The American Dream," lends itself to a writing assignment in which students examine Douglass's ideas and describe how his life and writing are relevant to a discussion of the American Dream.

Among the natural components of a unit on the American dream are the ideas and values of early American political leaders and of early and contemporary American writers, as well as the hopes and dreams expressed by immigrants. It's also valuable to talk about students' own views of what is good about America and what hopes are still unfulfilled.

Before students begin reading Douglass's *Narrative,* ask them to list ideas that make up the concept of the American Dream, as the class has discussed it so far, and write their ideas on the board.

Students' suggestions are likely to include freedom from persecution or oppression, freedom from government intrusion, choosing your own work and where to live, being able to say what you want, valuing individuality, tolerance of others, being able to raise a family in safety, knowing that your children will have an education, and so on. Ask students to keep these in mind as they begin reading Douglass's *Narrative.*

Also ask students to keep track of passages that seem particularly significant to them. When students have finished their reading, these passages may be shared as a class. For example, a student might read aloud a short passage from the section where Douglass describes "the turning-point in my career as a slave."

> This battle with Mr. Covey was the turning-point in my career as a slave. It rekindled the few expiring embers of freedom and revived within me a sense of my own manhood. It recalled the departed self-confidence and inspired me again with a determination to be free. This gratification afforded by the triumph was a full compensation for whatever else might follow, even death itself. . . . I now resolved that, however long I might remain a slave in form, the day had passed forever when I could be a slave in fact.

Common themes will arise among the passages that students bring up; this is a natural point to move from this discussion into a short lesson on the typical elements of a slave narrative. The slave narrative was a popular literary form during the eighteenth and nineteenth centuries, and Douglass was considered an extremely talented orator and journalist. Common features of slave narratives include the following points, which may be listed on the board:

- the use of abundant detail, to prove the writer's truthfulness
- a demonstration of white religious hypocrisy
- examples of the cruel practice of separating slave families
- instances of miscegenation—marriage or cohabitation between races
- the theme of a divided consciousness, caused in part by miscegenation and the loss of family ties
- the use of literacy as a means of obtaining freedom
- the theme of "freedom or death!"
- examples of the slave manifesting a higher level of morality than the white slave owners
- the suggestion that slavery corrupts the white slave owner as much as it destroys the life of the slave

Next, ask students to divide into six or eight small groups and to spend 15 to 20 minutes finding passages from Douglass's writing that illustrate these characteristics. Then reconvene the class and give each group a few minutes to share the best examples.

At this point, introduce the writing assignment. Students are to write a one- to two-page paper in which they examine how Frederick Douglass's life and *Narrative* are relevant to a discussion of the American Dream.

To help students get their ideas flowing, they might be asked to consider questions like "How does Douglass's work contribute to your view of American history?" "How can you resolve your picture of America and of the American Dream with the hypocrisy and horror that Douglass depicts?" "In what way did Douglass's life stand in contrast to specific ideals of the American Dream discussed in class?" "In what way did his struggles and achievements reinforce these same ideals and inspire others not to give up?" "What possibilities and promises suggested by the ideas of the American Dream, and pointed to in Douglass's struggles, are yet to be fulfilled?"

Students may choose to respond to questions like these, as long as they relate specific ideas and quotations from Douglass's writing to specific components of the American Dream.

The reading and discussion of Douglass's writing set the stage for some serious thinking on students' part; the writing assignment is likely to result in thoughtful, heartfelt papers and prompt further class discussion.

*Adapted from an idea by Jill Melancon, Norcross High School, Norcross, Georgia*

## Students Help Huck Finn Sing the Blues

As a graduate student about to begin my preservice teaching, I told my cooperating teacher that I wanted to make lessons with serious objectives fun for my students. Now, as I reflect on my preservice teaching, I'd like to share one lesson in particular in which I think this goal was achieved. I believe that the seed for this lesson was planted in my mind by pages 131–36 of Tom Romano's book *Clearing the Way: Working with Teenage Writers* (Heinemann, 1987).

I used this lesson with eleventh graders after they read Chapter 31 of *The Adventures of Huckleberry Finn,* but I think that it could be used with many different grade levels and with any literary work in which the protagonist struggles with himself or herself while contemplating an important decision. The activity takes three or four class periods to complete.

In Chapter 31 of *The Adventures of Huckleberry Finn*, Huck is torn between wanting to reveal the whereabouts of his traveling partner and best friend, Jim, a runaway slave, and wanting to be a good friend to Jim. I wanted to give my students the opportunity to explore Huck's dilemma in a creative and personal way. It occurred to me that the musical genre of the blues seemed to lend itself to this type of exploration, and that's how this lesson came about.

In introducing this assignment, I read to my students a paraphrase of a Mark Twain quotation: "Huck Finn is a book of mine where a sound heart and a deformed conscience come into collision and conscience suffers defeat." Then I asked them to think of one connection between this quotation and Chapter 31 of the novel. After a few minutes, I asked for volunteers to share their answers. During this discussion, we defined the literary concepts of *main conflict* and *climax* and explored how they manifest themselves in Chapter 31.

Once this discussion was completed, I had intended to use the overhead projector to make a chart with my students showing the reasons why Huck wants, and does not want, to turn Jim in, but time constraints prevented this. Some teachers might want to include this chart-making exercise, or perhaps students could tackle it on their own.

During the next class period, I explained to students that their assignment would be to write a blues song from Huck's perspective, in which they examined the reasons why Huck wants to turn Jim in, as well as the reasons why he wants Jim to remain free. Students would be free to write a blues song from Jim's perspective as well, but because Huck is the narrator of Twain's book, readers are more tuned in to Huck's thoughts and emotions than to Jim's. Still, the character of Jim clearly had his own struggles, and imaginative students who were interested in tackling blues songs from the perspectives of both Huck and Jim were encouraged to do so.

To provide some background, I explained that blues is a music form that started in the rural South among African Americans and is an expression of, as well as an attempt to transcend, a melancholy spirit.

I visited the Blues Foundation Web site (http://www.blues.org) to obtain more information about the blues. According to the current Web site, the blues is a musical style "created in response to the hardships endured by generations of African American people." It "descended from earlier work shouts" and "is primarily a vocal narrative style featuring solo voice with instrumental accompaniment." As African Americans migrated from rural areas to urban areas, "blues gradually became more of an urban phenomenon." It also became popular among white musicians. In the 1950s, "rhythm and blues hits were often rerecorded ('covered') by musicians such as Elvis Presley and Bill Haley, transforming rhythm and blues into rock and roll." (Much more information, including lists of recommended books and CDs, is available on the Blues Foundation Web site.)

I played an audiocassette of a blues song by Robert Johnson entitled "Walkin' Blues." I displayed the lyrics on the overhead projector while the song was playing. (These lyrics can be found at http:// xroads.virginia.edu/~MUSIC/blues/wb.html.)

Then, modeling a blues song from the point of view of another literary character experiencing personal struggle, I share with students a song that I wrote from the perspective of Shakespeare's Hamlet. Here's an excerpt from "The To-Be-or-Not-To-Be Blues":

Oh, I got those to-be-or-not-to-be blues
My mother, you see, married the snake
who murdered my father, the king
And the king, to further complicate this thing,
Chose me (Me! Why oh why did he have to choose me?)
to make sure the new, slithery king pays his dues
That is, I have to see to it that he sheds his mortal skin.
Oh, I got those to-be-or-not-to-be blues

Students were then inspired to begin work on their own blues songs. I established the following criteria for the assignment:

1. Length (2 stanzas of 5 lines each): 10 points
2. Originality/creativity: 10 points
3. Vernacular (choosing words and diction to suit the character's voice): 10 points
4. Two reasons why Huck wants to turn Jim in: 10 points each
5. Two reasons why Huck does not want to turn Jim in: 10 points each
6. What Huck decides to do: 10 points
7. Title: 10 points

8. Presentation: 10 points
Total: 100 points

Students had the rest of the class period to begin writing their songs and then finished them as homework. During the following class period, students presented their blues songs aloud to their peers. We created a coffeehouse atmosphere by moving the desks together in sets of twos and threes and by placing these sets of desks at odd angles around a stool that sat in the middle of the room. I had Robert Johnson blues songs playing in the background as students entered the room.

The presentations of the blues songs were a lot of fun. Some students sang their songs, and one student even tried to provide accompaniment on a harmonica that I had brought in. One student indicated that the assignment expanded her creativity, and another student stated that it was more interactive than just reading the book.

This assignment called on students to analyze textual material and to synthesize it in a creative way. I believe that it challenged students intellectually and allowed them to have fun at the same time.

Here is an example of a blues song written by one of my students. I greatly enjoy the literary skill and understanding of Huck's character that it displays:

### The Which-Way-to-Choose Blues

There is a friend named Jim, who's giving me the blues
Ya see he's a run away slave and that's bad news
I really don't know what to do
My conscience tells me to give him up, but if I do I'll be a shrew
Slaves are just like whites ya see.

An I really think they should be free
But slaves are the white owner's property
An I would be steeln from them
It's risky business travln with a slave
If I can dare to be brave, I would be treated as a knave.

I stops for a moment and rips up the letter
Cause I thinks to myself that Jim deserves better.

*From a teacher in New York State who wishes to remain anonymous*

## Active Learning Ideas

In *Active Learning,* Mel Silberman says, "When learning is active, students do most of the work. They use their brains . . . studying ideas, solving problems, and applying what they learn. Active learning is fast-paced, fun, supportive, and personally engaging" (p. ix).

In the past year I've become interested in active-learning techniques and have found the following to be useful sources on this topic:

*Active Learning: 101 Strategies to Teach Any Subject* by Mel Silberman (Allyn and Bacon, 1996)

*"You Gotta BE the Book"* by Jeff Wilhelm (NCTE, 1997)

*Imagining to Learn: Inquiry, Ethics, and Integration through Drama* by Jeff Wilhelm and B. Eminston (Heinemann, 1998)

*Promoting Active Learning: Strategies for the College Classroom* by C. Meyers and T. B. Jones (Josey-Bass, 1993)

Drawing from these sources, I've used the techniques described below to engage students more actively in the study and enjoyment of literature.

## Setting the Stage

To pique students' interest and to prepare them for reading a novel, I asked them to do some background research on the time period in which the novel takes place and to prepare a presentation to the class. The first novel with which I used this idea was *The Things They Carried* by Tim O'Brien. Since the novel is about the Vietnam War, I asked my juniors to form pairs and to research topics ranging from the Vietnam Veterans Memorial Wall to the use of Agent Orange and napalm. After students did their research, each pair prepared a five-minute presentation, giving the whole class the benefit of their knowledge.

I used this same project with *A Separate Peace* by John Knowles. This novel is set at a private preparatory school during WWII, so students had a choice of researching such topics as General MacArthur and war bonds.

This activity worked well with both novels. The background information seemed to help students connect with the novel and understand what was happening to the characters.

## Talk Show

With me as the host, the class pretended we were conducting a talk show involving the characters in the play *The Glass Menagerie* by Tennessee Williams. The activity began by having the students brainstorm a variety of questions they would like to ask these characters. Then I asked for three volunteers to come to the front of the room and play the roles of Amanda, Tom, and Laura Wingfield.

The other students asked questions of the characters, and the characters responded. Typical questions were "Tom, why did you leave your mom and sister?" and "Laura, what is so great about those glass figurines?"

This activity was effective because the students asked questions that dealt with character motivations and deeper issues in the play, and both the questioning and the answering involved careful thought and using knowledge and understanding gained from reading.

## Choral Reading

Another idea I tried was choral reading. I used this with the novel *The Catcher in the Rye* by J. D. Salinger. First, to focus students' attention on the emotions and voices of Holden and his mother, I asked students to pretend they were one of these two characters and to write a letter to the other character expressing their feelings.

Next I handed out cards of two different colors (one for Holden and one for his mother). Students were asked to create one line of text that was the epitome of what the particular character wanted to say to the other character, and to write it on their card.

Then students met in groups according to their character, read their lines aloud, and selected the three best lines. The writers of the top three lines from each group stood at the front of the room and read their lines aloud, alternating between Holden and his mother.

Finally, I asked the students at the front of the room to take turns reading their lines as if reading one continuous poem. Afterward, I asked the class how they thought the poem sounded and if any of the lines should be moved around for better effect. We made some adjustments and tried it a few times. Because the lines were in the voices of Holden and his mother, the impromptu poem took on the character of a conversation between them.

## Using Drama to Review

With one novel, *A Separate Peace* by John Knowles, many of my students expressed concern over not remembering what happened in the beginning of the book, so I used this method for helping them review events. I visited the Web site at http://www.novelguide.com and found summaries for the chapters from the book. These summaries are much like *Cliffs Notes;* however, they are free.

I printed one chapter summary for each group, who then had a day in which to prepare a skit for the class based on the chapter summary. The groups did a great job. Some students brought in Barbie dolls to play the roles, and others brought in stuffed animals for a puppet show. Most groups, however, chose to act out the characters themselves and to have one person be the narrator. Overall, students had fun with this activity and reviewed the novel in the process.

I believe these activities helped increase my students' involvement and comprehension in their reading, and the enthusiastic responses I received demonstrated to me that these and other active-learning techniques are worth trying again.

*Kelli Donais, Eastview High School, Apple Valley, Minnesota*

---

# Comparing Two Works of Mystery Fiction

---

Students often balk at writing a paper because, they claim, they don't know what to write about. After our class has read Arthur Conan Doyle's "The Speckled Band" and Edgar Allan Poe's "Murders in the Rue Morgue," I use the following activity to head off this situation and get students warmed up for a paper assignment comparing the two works.

I devote a class period to small-group discussion of the literature in question. Working in groups of about four, students discuss a topic that lends itself to a functional thesis statement. (The thesis itself is developed later on, perhaps in the next class.)

To begin, I usually assign each group a topic or let each group choose one of these four topics: *greed, literary techniques, character/*

*personality,* and *justice.* Here are sample discussion questions for the small groups to use as prompts to stimulate thinking and discussion. (You could distribute all of these questions or select three or four for each topic.)

1. Discuss the theme of *greed.* Consider some or all of the following questions:

    What kind of role does greed play in society?

    Does this role change over the years, or does it seem to be a standard, unchanging part of human nature?

    How do you see human greed affecting the lives of characters in Doyle's and Poe's stories?

    Do you think greed as a motive makes the crimes believable? Why?

    Could the same situations happen today?

    Would you find these stories believable if you read them as true accounts in a recent newspaper from *[insert your town's name]?*

    Answer as many of these questions as you need to (or create your own questions) in order to fully develop your topic of greed.

2. Discuss Doyle's and Poe's *literary techniques.* For instance, you could cite examples from the stories that create a feeling of suspense in readers or that create realistic environments and dialogue to produce believable stories.

    How is Poe's style different from Doyle's?

    Why do you think these writers' stories are still popular even after more than a century?

    Why do you think readers are interested in tales of murder and mystery?

    Do you think writers such as Doyle and Poe created this interest in crime and mystery, or do you think they were responding to an interest that people already had?

3. Discuss the *characters* of Sherlock Holmes and Dupin. Cite evidence from the stories to show what their personalities are like, what their characteristic actions and opinions are, and how they tend to view life and death.

How do they relate to their assistants, Watson and the unnamed narrator of Poe's story?

Are they good leaders? How do they interact with other characters? What else do you see in these characters?

Remember that characters become real through action, dialogue, and description, so try to draw examples from all three areas. You could focus your discussion as a comparison and contrast of the two detectives, or you could focus on only one detective.

4. Discuss the theme of *justice* in Doyle's and Poe's stories. Consider some of the following questions:

Do you think that justice is achieved in Doyle's story?

Read the last sentence of the story; what is Holmes's opinion of Roylott's death? What are your opinions of Holmes's comment?

What other stories have you read in which a villain's scheme backfires and the villain is hurt by his or her own plan to hurt others? Why do you think this is a particularly satisfying conclusion to a story about crime?

Do you think justice is achieved in the end in the story by Poe? Why or why not?

People tend to disagree over the justice of Poe's ending more than they do regarding Doyle's, so be sure to explain your line of thought carefully.

Students discuss these questions within their groups, voicing opinions, sharing ideas, and simply being heard. I encourage everyone to take notes and to use the notes later to help generate ideas for a paper.

I ask each group to share one or two (or three, depending on time constraints) of the most interesting or surprising or ingenious ideas they came up with. The rest of the class takes notes on what these students say, further developing their own idea base for a paper. I've noticed that the practice of having students take notes on one another's comments encourages pride and self-confidence in the students and fosters a personal connection to the writing project.

I let the students see me taking notes on what they are saying; moreover, I use individual students' names as frequently as possible when I moderate these sharing sessions and again in later classes when I refer to what individuals said.

Finally, during the last five minutes of class, students freewrite individually on what they think will be the topic for their own paper. Each student leaves the class with a wealth of ideas for the paper, and each student has broken the barrier of the blank page.

*Lesli J. Favor, Dallas, Texas*

# *3* Explorations

The teaching ideas in this final chapter provide a variety of ways to motivate students and promote learning in the English classroom. Included are read-around-groups, letter writing, making sense of nonsense, and conducting research and interviews. In these activities, students design their own learning experience, read with an adult partner, explore career options, shake out the cobwebs with movement, and participate in a poetry slam.

## What I Want to Learn

One aspect of educational reform has been to focus a great deal of attention on the empowerment of students. In that vein, I have designed (with help from Tom Gregory) the What I Want to Learn assignment. It takes approximately four weeks to complete, including the final exhibitions.

I distribute the following student handout and tell students that I am going to give them the opportunity to design their own learning experience. Each student will select a topic of particular interest to him or her and will determine how to obtain information about that topic.

After students have put together a well-crafted proposal, they begin their discovery of their new interest. During the study, I meet with the students weekly to discuss their progress and their plans for exhibiting what they have learned. Obviously, I have to coordinate with the librarian, local specialists, and various agencies in the community to facilitate the students' gathering of information they need to fulfill their study. Every time I have done this, the task has gotten a little easier.

Student exhibitions have been innovative. One student studied how to repair his motorcycle. He learned how to take the engine apart, put it back together, and actually get it to work. His demonstration was to take the carburetor apart, replace the gaskets, and put it back together in class. It was an excellent presentation.

Two other students decided they wanted to learn how to fence—not with posts, but with foils, épées, and sabers. Neither of them spoke French, but they discovered they would need to know French terms in order to learn how to fence. They built wooden swords, put together fencing outfits using materials they had available, and demonstrated a fencing competition for the class. At the end of their exhibition, most of their classmates wanted to try fencing as well.

As you can see, the sky is the limit for this assignment. It involves a great deal of personal discipline on the part of the students, but the risks are worth it. Additionally, to make the exhibitions successful, students must display personal initiative and creativity—skills we all need to work on.

## What I Want to Learn—An Independent Study

Can you think of a single time in your school careers when you have been given the opportunity to learn about something that really interests you? If you are like most of us, someone else has always told you what and when to learn.

I'd like to change that by giving you the chance to design your own learning experience as part of this class during the next nine weeks.

Why is this important? I believe doing a project such as this gives you a chance to better understand what it means to learn something new and how much work will be involved to learn this new skill or topic well.

Are you ready for the responsibility that goes along with a project like this? I believe you are, and I look forward to talking with each of you about what you'd like to learn.

Beyond choosing what skill or information you will learn, you will also have the opportunity to decide how you will learn this and how you will demonstrate your new knowledge. In a condensed form, that's your assignment.

Now, what skill or information would you like to learn? My only suggestion here is to make sure you pick something you can get excited about. Otherwise, you'll find yourself regretting having to work on the project. So choose something you can really get into.

After we talk about what you'd like to learn, you need to write up a proposal for your learning experience. The proposal should contain a minimum of three sections:

1. What I want to learn is _____ and why.
2. This is how I plan to learn about it.
3. This is how I will demonstrate what I have learned.

Go into as much detail as you can in each section. Also, share this assignment with others. Your classmates, your families, and your friends may have suggestions about how to learn about this topic.

One warning—don't rely on someone else to decide what and how you will learn. This is your project, so each one of you should make it your own.

Good luck and happy learning!

*Ted Baechtold, Eastern High School, Bloomfield, Indiana*

## Read with Me

I began using this idea after hearing it described at a county inservice by David Winter of Wheeler High School. Students pair up with adults to read and evaluate a book. Students and their reading partners each write a review, with the two generations sometimes reaching different conclusions. I encourage the pairs to discuss the book and to determine where they agree and where they disagree. Then students make a presentation of the two reviews and provide any insights they have about the differing viewpoints.

Not only does this activity work well, but I have had parents contact me about how pleased they were to have an opportunity to work jointly with their children. Parents have related how dinner-table discussions revolve around the book they are reading, and in some cases both parents have read the book and written a critique.

In addition to parents, I have had students read with a youth minister, a neighbor, or a grandparent. I set an age minimum for the adult since I want students to get the perspective of someone older than themselves. I realize adults can't always adhere to the time frame of our classroom, so students are not penalized if the adult review is missing when the presentation is made—but it's important for each adult to eventually submit a review. Be sure to have a couple of adult volunteers lined up to be a partner with any students whose parents are unable to participate.

Here is the handout that I give to students.

### Read with Me Project

For this parallel reading, you must find an adult who will agree to read the same book as you. You and your partner will read the book and then rate it according to a system you (the student) have devised. Next, you will both write a review of the book. Finally, you will make a presentation of the book incorporating both reviews and ratings.

Here are the steps:

1. Begin by finding a reading partner—a parent or other adult relative is ideal, but consider other adults as well (a minister or church group leader, a coach, a scout leader, a neighbor, a teacher, a co-worker). Your reading partner should be at least _____ years old. Then select a book to read. The adult can be active in the book selection, or you can decide which book you'd like to read. Turn in the name of the adult who is your reading partner and the title of the book you have decided upon.

2. After completion of the book, two reviews are written: one by your adult reading partner and one by you, the student. Your review counts twice as much as your reading partner's review because it will be graded for grammar and composition skills as well as content. Basically, you will get the points for your partner's review simply by it being in the project.

3. The reviews are attached to poster board to make a visual display. The poster can be as small as a half sheet of poster board or as large as a full-sized piece of poster board. The area should be divided into three parts: on the left is your reading partner's review and rating; in the center is the bibliographic information and a mock-up of the original cover design of the book; on the right is your review and rating. You must devise a rating system for you and your reading partner that is pertinent to your book— 5 stars or "thumbs up/down" is not acceptable. Be ingenious!

4. The final step is oral presentation of the poster and the book. Your reading partner is certainly welcome to participate in this part of the project, but his or her presence is not required.

Please note that your responsibility is to read the book, develop a rating system, write your review, create your presentation, and present it to the class. Your deadline is _____. Hopefully, your reading partner will have his or her part of the project completed and ready to go on time; however, whether or not that review is completed by _____, yours must be turned in then in order to escape a late penalty.

The steps contribute to your project grade as follows:

Step 1:  5%
Step 2:  60% (40%/20%)
Step 3:  25%
Step 4:  10%

*Keyna Cabrera, Pope High School, Marietta, Georgia*

---

# The Grammar of Nonsense

I use a paragraph I wrote to encourage my students midway through our study of grammar. I hand out the following passage to students and ask them to answer the two questions:

## Lunt and Cloppey

Lunt and Cloppey were bumples.  One flavel Lunt and Cloppey were flogging to brank.  Clopey stiled some of Lunt's claggers since el couldn't trub els. Lunt was quite groupy and rombled, "Munk me my claggers!" At that, Cloppey plarked Lunt; and the bumples twerted to flent, crinkling into the moll.  Blarkly, Lunt's moop terrined, ella stuped each bumple and glossed ellem tunk, both slarbing all the way.

1.  What two things did Blarkly do to Lunt and Cloppey?

2. What did Cloppey do when Lunt rombled?

Students are, of course, baffled by the vocabulary and consequently the meaning of the passage. However, when I ask them about the grammatical roles of the various words in this passage, they discover to their surprise that they can work out the answers, in terms of what words seem to be nouns, pronouns, and proper nouns, what words are acting as verbs, and so on. This exercise serves as a brief and pleasant diversion, as well as a confidence booster for my seventh graders, since they find out that they already know more than they thought they did.

*June Bell, Liberty Junior High School, West Chester, Ohio*

## Career Inquiries

To help my students learn about career options and gain real-world writing practice, I ask them to write to a person in a career in which they have an interest. They have several days to consider various occupations, to find someone working in that career (or retired from that career) to whom to write, and to obtain the correct address to use.

We brainstorm as a class to help students think up sources for their research. If students or their parents don't personally know a person in the selected career, other students and teachers in related areas can often supply names. If all else fails, we have found that sources acquired through the phone book or the Internet respond at a rate comparable to people with whom the students are acquainted.

I caution students about writing to celebrities, who most likely won't reply to their specific questions, but we have received gratifying responses from such varied professionals as a local news anchor, the directors of a major observatory and a famous aquarium, a noted homicide detective, and doctors in numerous specialties.

With the added motivation of contacting a real person, students are receptive to studying the appropriate format for business-style letters. We review the basics, and I ask students to format the main section of their letters as a list of six to ten questions. Some might be taken from a generic list we generate in class, while others might be adaptations of those or questions the students fashion themselves. In the conclusion, the students request a reply by a certain date and express their gratitude.

To ensure that the letters follow business-letter format and are mechanically perfect, students proofread one another's letters in peer groups, and then I peruse them, returning ones that still need revision. I mail the final letters, which the students have inserted into stamped, addressed envelopes that also include stamped, self-addressed envelopes for the replies.

Then we wait expectantly. Most students receive detailed responses, and some enjoy full packets of information or invitations to visit a job site. Frequently the letters contain suggestions regarding high school courses or volunteer opportunities that would be useful preparation for a given job or career. (Of course, I enthusiastically reinforce any advice concerning the importance of English-related skills!)

Occasionally, a letter prompts a student to reconsider a career choice, but I always recommend that students investigate further before basing any decisions on one inquiry.

Besides the obvious practical benefits of this assignment, I have found there are auxiliary advantages. Not to be overlooked, for example, is the subtle message that most people do have to work hard for a living, and that the more consideration a person gives to what they actually enjoy doing and what they do well, the more likely it is that they will find a satisfying job or career. Another byproduct is the forging of school-community ties and the thrill students feel when a busy, accomplished adult takes an interest in them.

I like to make this assignment a supplement to a study of *Great Expectations.* I use it at the point in the story when Pip receives the news of his great expectations (Chapter 18). The novel's theme of self-fulfillment ties in neatly with the goal of the activity, and students are able to identify even more with Pip after spending some time considering their own quest for meaningful work and a place in the world.

*Ellen Janis, Cedar City, Utah*

## Get Out There and Move Something

We've gone to 4 x 4 block scheduling, so I have 90-minute classes with my students. As a result, I've tried to think of ways to incorporate movement in my classes to help keep both their interest and blood flowing.

One thing I do is mark the four corners of the room with the following labels: *Strongly  Agree, Agree, Strongly Disagree,* and *Disagree.* I then read a statement, and the students move to whichever corner of the room corresponds to their thoughts. To keep them from just following their friends, I ask one or two why they strongly agree or disagree with the statement.

This idea about the four corners was given to me at an inservice years ago, and I have adapted it to my own purposes. For instance, when teaching the story "American History" by Judith Ortiz Cofer, I read aloud various statements about prejudice and ask students to indicate agreement or disagreement by picking a corner of the room.

I also try to incorporate movement when the students work in small groups. I develop groups of related words and tape a different word on the back of each student's shirt. They walk around asking yes or no questions about their word until they figure out which students have related words and, thus, form a group.

I use different group types each time. For instance, one time I might use groups of words that relate to works of literature we've studied; another time, words that relate to types of foods; and another, words that relate to periods of history.

*Lisa M. Hamilton, Morgan County High School, Madison, Georgia*

---

# Classroom Poetry Slam

A poetry slam is an event involving two or more poets competing before a live audience. Olympics-style judging is conducted by selected members of the audience. The performances generally involve a mixture of poetry, theater, and stand-up comedy. Audience participation and reaction to the poems are encouraged, but students are reminded that this is a *friendly* competition.

The first official poetry slam took place in 1986 in Chicago. Poetry slams are now regularly held in over 30 U.S. cities. The 1999 National Poetry Slam, which attracted hundreds of competing poets, was held in Chicago. Visit http://www.poetryslam.com for more information.

Over the last three years, I have organized six poetry slam workshop sessions at the Young Writers' Conference held annually at

Cornell College in Mt. Vernon, Iowa, and sponsored by the Grant Wood Area Education Agency.

The conference is attended by junior high and high school students in the region served by the agency. The poetry slams take place in the course of the 65-minute workshop slots, although one could more easily imagine the process occurring over the length of two class periods: one 50-minute class period for setting up the schedule and assignments, and the next class period for the actual poetry slam.

In order to participate in the poetry slam, a student writes his or her name on a piece of paper and tosses it into the hat. The first eight names pulled from the hat are the performers; the next five names pulled from the hat are the judges. If enough students are interested, there could be two sets of judges, one for the first round and another for the second and final rounds.

The eight performers are grouped into four pairs. In Round 1, each pair of competitors squares off for a match involving the reading and performing of one poem of limited length (up to three minutes or two pages). The judges rate each poem on a scale of 1 (a poem that totally bombs) to 10 (a poem that is "da bomb"). The highest and lowest scores are dropped, and the three middle scores are added together for a total score.

The four Round 1 winners advance to Round 2, and the two Round 2 winners advance to Round 3, the final round. The winner of that round is acknowledged as the Poetry Slam Champion. I always give that person some sort of award or prize.

A few general comments are appropriate here. The judging of one's poems by one's peers can be a little traumatic for some young writers. I make sure to tune in to the feelings of the readers (and the judges) and give everyone a lot of support and encouragement.

Some class time can also be spent helping the students establish their judging criteria (rubrics). I help them decide to what extent they are judging the poem and to what extent the performance. I also emphasize the playful side of the poetry slam format. Although poetry slams are designed as competitions, the competition aspect is, in practice, not taken very seriously.

In the slams I've organized, I've found that high school students appreciate the fact that they are being evaluated by their peers. The judging aspect has always been viewed as positive and constructive.

During the various breaks between the matches and the rounds, the judges and other nonparticipants are given the opportunity to read one of their own poems. We playfully refer to these as "intermissions" or "commercial breaks."

If you use a poetry slam as the culminating event of a poetry-writing unit, you might encourage or require those students who are less comfortable performing their poems before the class to "publish" one poem in a broadside format that could then be posted in the classroom. These poems could be illustrated, hand-printed on high-quality paper or cardstock, or designed and printed on a computer.

***David Duer, Iowa City, Iowa***

# Indexes

## Author Index

## Subject Index